O7-BSN-104

The Holocaust

Charles George

KIDHAVEN
PRESS™

THOMSON
GALE

San Diego • Detroit • New York • San Francisco • Cleveland
New Haven, Conn. • Waterville, Maine • London • Munich

THOMSON
GALE

On cover: Former prisoners walk away from the Buchenwald concentration camp after being liberated by U.S. Army troops in 1945.

Cover photo: Associated Press, AP
Associated Press, AP, 28, 40
Associated Press, Files, 42
Associated Press, The Herald-Dispatch, 29
Associated Press, U.S. Army Signal Corps, 20
© Bettmann/CORBIS, 22, 38
© CORBIS, 14, 31
© James David/CORBIS SYGMA, 32
© Christel Gerstenberg/CORBIS, 9
© Dave G. Houser/CORBIS, 18
© Hulton/Archive by Getty Images, 37
Library of Congress, 6, 35
National Archives, 5, 24
Brandy Noon, 12, 21
Simon Wiesenthal Center, 10, 26

For more information, contact
KidHaven Press
27500 Drake Rd.
Farmington Hills, MI 48331-3535
Or you can visit our Internet site at http://www.gale.com

LIBRARY OF CONGRESS CATALOGING-IN-PUBLICATION DATA

George, Charles.
  The Holocaust / by Charles George.
    p. cm.—(History of the world series)
Summary: Discusses Hitler's plan to exterminate the Jews, life in the camps, resistance of the prisoners, and the topics of freedom, justice, and the remembrance of those who died.
Includes bibliographical references (p.) and index.
  ISBN 0-7377-1382-8 (hardback : alk. paper)
  1. Holocaust, Jewish (1939–1945)—Juvenile literature. [1. Holocaust, Jewish (1939–1945)] I. Title. II. Series.
  D804.34 .G46 2003
  940 .53'18—dc21

                                                           2002004511

Printed in China

Contents

Introduction
Hitler's Plan

From 1933 to 1945, just before and during World War II, Nazi Germany murdered more than 6 million Jews. Nazi Germany also murdered millions of other people they felt were inferior or dangerous: Gypsies, Jehovah's Witnesses, priests, ministers, homosexuals, and the disabled. This carefully planned, government-sponsored massacre is called the Holocaust.

Jews were not killed because they had committed crimes. They were not killed because they had planned to overthrow the government. They were put to death because they were Jews. Adolf Hitler, the leader of Nazi Germany blamed the Jews for Germany's social and economic problems. He felt Jews were not true Germans, that they were spoiling Germany's racial purity.

Hitler hated Jews, but he was not the first person to feel that way. Many early Christians blamed Jews for the death of Jesus Christ. Because of this, **anti-**

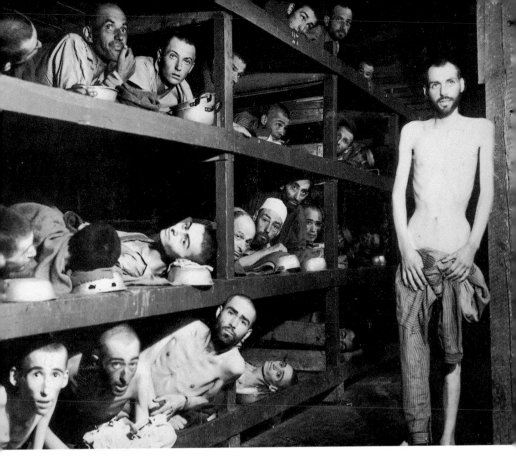

Starving concentration camp prisoners squeeze into tight sleeping quarters.

Semitic, or anti-Jewish, feelings were common in Europe. Hitler made clear his hatred of Jews eleven years before coming to power. He told a friend, "If I am ever really in power, the destruction of the Jews will be my first and most important job."[1]

The Final Solution

When Hitler was named leader of Germany in 1933, he began a program to rid Germany of its 525,000 Jews. First, he passed laws making it hard for Jews to make a living or to practice their religion. He believed this would force Jews to leave the country. Many did. Others could not afford to leave, or could not find another country that would accept them. These Jews were forced to stay in Germany. Still others thought Nazi rule would pass, and that life would return to normal. These Jews chose to stay.

Nazis stand guard while Adolf Hilter explains the new rules for Jews at a rally in Germany.

When Germany invaded Poland in 1939, and the Soviet Union in 1941, Hitler began the second step in his program. He wanted Jews to live apart from non-Jews. He ordered millions of Jews into **ghettos**, or walled-in neighborhoods. Rounding them up in ghettos made it easy to get rid of them.

His third step, the **Final Solution**, as Nazis called it, was a carefully guarded secret. Nazis built camps in Germany and eastern Europe for the mass execution of Jews. In these camps, called concentration camps, Jews would be worked, starved, beaten, hanged, shot, gassed, and burned. All these actions were taken in the name of racial purity. In other words, Hitler wanted to rid the world of Jews.

One-Way Ticket to the Camps

Hitler's program against the Jews began slowly. Little by little, from 1933 until 1939, he made life difficult for them. Eventually, he made life for the Jews impossible.

Anti-Jewish Laws

Early Nazi laws took away many Jewish rights and freedoms. Their businesses were closed, their books and important papers burned, and their **synagogues** (or places of worship) destroyed. They were forced to carry special papers to identify themselves as Jews. They also had to wear yellow stars marked *Jude*, German for Jew, on their clothes.

Before Hitler became the leader, Jews worked in all kinds of jobs. But under Nazi rule, Jews were thrown out of schools and universities. They were barred from holding jobs in medicine, banking, law, and government. They could not marry non-Jews.

They could not visit public places, such as parks or swimming pools. They could not own dogs, radios, or weapons. In only a few years, Nazi Germany

An anti-Semitic document begins "When you see this sign . . ." and bears the gold star that all Jews were forced to wear.

turned Jews into second-class citizens. Then, in 1935 the Nuremberg Laws also took away their citizenship. Without citizenship, Jews could not vote. Without the vote, Jews were powerless.

The First Concentration Camps

With more than four hundred anti-Jewish laws, it became impossible for Jews not to break a law. Once arrested, they usually went to prison without a trial. With so many people to put into prison, Hitler ordered camps built to "concentrate" those Germans he considered dangerous: Jews, real criminals, and political prisoners who opposed Hitler's actions.

As Jews line the sidewalk, a Jewish policeman patrols a ghetto street.

On March 22, 1933, six years before World War II began, Nazis opened the first of these camps—Dachau—near Munich, in southern Germany. Nazis opened another camp, Sachsenhausen, just outside Berlin, in September 1936. In the summer of 1937, the Buchenwald concentration camp opened near Weimar, in central Germany.

To these camps, and to others, the Nazis sent thousands of prisoners. Every prisoner received harsh treatment—backbreaking work, poor food, unheated housing, and cruel punishment—but Jews were singled out. By the time German forces invaded Poland on September 1, 1939, beginning World War II, thousands of people occupied Germany's prison camps.

Once Poland came under Nazi control, Hitler had to deal with 3.3 million Polish Jews. More camps had to be built. By 1945, at the end of the war, Nazis had built twenty-three main concentration camps in Germany and Poland. Most of these larger camps had smaller camps attached to them. Many of the one thousand smaller camps housed factories. The factories used forced labor to produce items for the German army.

Life in the Ghettos

While these camps were being built, Jews were imprisoned in ghettos in the nation's major cities, including Warsaw and Lodz. The ghettos were built in the cities for two reasons. Nazis wanted to rid the

Major Concentration Camps

North Sea

Baltic Sea

Neuengamme

Ravensbrück

Bergen-Belsen   Sachsenhausen

GERMANY

Chelmno

Treblinka

POLAND

Buchenwald

Majdanek

Sobibor

Theresienstadt

Auschwitz

Belzec

CZECHOSLOVAKIA

Dachau

Mauthausen

AUSTRIA

● Large-scale labor camps
□ Large-scale extermination camps

Adriatic
Sea

Mediterranean
Sea

surrounding countryside of Jews to make room for German settlement. Nazis also wanted Jews near major railways, where it would be easy to send them to concentration camps.

Conditions were harsh in the ghettos. In the Warsaw ghetto a half million Jews were crowded into an area of only 3.5 square miles. Surrounding them was an eleven-foot-high brick wall topped with broken glass. Starvation, extreme cold, illness, and overwork in forced labor gangs killed thousands. Ten percent died in the first year.

The cruel living conditions were not the worst thing about the ghetto. Nazis came to the ghettos each day for "selection." They announced that some Jews were to be moved to other labor camps, where conditions were better. This was a lie. They sold Jews third-class train tickets, and told them to pack their belongings and bring enough money to last them for a few weeks. At first, the Nazis chose only the old, the young, the sick, and those no longer able to work. After a while, when they wanted to empty the ghettos, every Jew was "selected" for transport.

Author and Holocaust survivor Elie Wiesel saw the selection process firsthand, first in the ghetto that had once been his hometown, and later when he was sent to Auschwitz and Buchenwald. At the age of fifteen, he watched Jews in his neighborhood stand in sweltering heat in the street for hours awaiting selection. And then, he said, "They began their journey without a backward glance at the abandoned streets, the dead, empty houses, the gardens, the tombstones."[2] Some Jews seemed to know what lay ahead of them, but they went anyway. They felt they had nowhere to turn for help.

Transport to the Camps

Once Jews left the ghetto, they were herded into unheated railroad cattle cars and locked in for the trip. Each boxcar was crowded with sixty to one hundred people. Prisoners had to take turns sitting down. Sometimes they were locked in these cars without food, water, or toilets for a week or more. Many died. Those who survived the transports soon discovered they were not going to a better place. They were being sent to one of the death camps Nazis had built in Poland between 1942 and 1944.

Dead Jews lie face down in the rubble of the Warsaw ghetto after being brutally murdered.

In all, Nazis built six such camps—at Belzec, Sobibor, Treblinka, Chelmno, Majdanek, and Auschwitz-Birkenau. At these six camps, 3 million to 4 million people were murdered. No one knows the exact count. These camps were located in remote areas of Poland, to hide what they were being used for. The most deadly camp was Auschwitz-Birkenau. More than 1 million people were killed there with poison gas; their bodies were then burned in **crematory ovens**. Nine out of ten were Jews.

Chapter Two

Life and Death in the Camps

Each time a trainload of Jews arrived at a concentration camp, the routine was the same. The dead bodies of those who had not survived the trip were removed from the boxcars. The survivors were ordered to line up. Most stumbled out, too weak, hungry, and filthy to resist. Some did not know what was about to happen to them. Others did. They had heard rumors of death camps where Jews were killed and their bodies burned. Smoke billowing from camp chimneys told them they were about to die.

Nazi officials wanted the process to run smoothly. In most camps, they tried to persuade newly arrived Jews that they had come to a new work camp. Some camps welcomed new arrivals with a band playing classical music. Others put up signs labeled TAILORS, CARPENTERS, and other professions, to make prisoners think there was work for them. In other camps, though, Nazis did not bother with such tricks.

Instead, they controlled their victims with brute force. In these camps, snarling dogs, yelling, whipping, and clubbing enforced order. Tall guard towers manned with machine guns, and ten-foot-tall electrified barbed wire fences told Jews they were trapped.

Camp Selections

In each camp, no matter how they had been greeted, Jews were forced to go through another selection. This time, Nazis separated men from women and children. Stronger men were put to work in camp factories. Older men, most women, and all children were sent directly to the place the Nazis called the showers. Nazi officials told them they were going to bathe. To those who did not know the truth of what was about to happen, a shower sounded wonderful after such a grueling train trip, so they went willingly. Others, who had guessed the showers were actually gas chambers, usually followed, too. Most were too weak to resist.

One Holocaust survivor, Ernst Michel, later described what happened when he arrived at Auschwitz:

> We were forced into two columns, women on one side, men on the other side. . . . At the end of the line there was an SS man [a Nazi officer] in a beautiful leather coat, and as we walked by he asked us, "How old?" If you were between the ages of sixteen and thirty, the thumb went up and you went to one side. Over thirty, the

Millions of Jews were sent to their deaths after passing through this entrance to Auschwitz. The sign translates to "Work will set you free."

thumb went down, and you went to the other side. . . . They piled us into trucks, and then a guard said something to me that I didn't understand. He said, "You're the lucky ones." I said, "What do you mean?" And he said, "The others are already up the chimney." That's when we started to realize what this place was.[3]

A Trip to the Showers

Even inside the pretend showers, Nazis tried to fool Jews into thinking everything was going to be all right. In dressing rooms, guards told Jews to undress, hang their clothes on numbered hooks (so they could find them after their shower), and take a towel and soap into the shower. In some camps, as many as two thousand Jews at a time were then herded into rooms with shower heads in the ceilings. Once the doors were closed and sealed, however, no water came through the shower heads. Instead, **Zyklon B**, a poison gas first used to kill rats, poured in. Within five minutes, everyone in the room was dead. The Nazis had tried other methods of killing, including shooting Jews one at a time and burying them in mass graves. More than one million Jews died this way. But the gas chambers were faster and easier than shooting and burying.

Once the poisonous fumes cleared, other camp prisoners entered the room and removed the dead. They shaved the bodies and searched them for gold teeth. Their hair was later used as insulation in German submarines, or made into felt boots. Gold from their teeth was melted down and poured into bars. Finally, workers dragged the bodies to huge pits for burial, or to special ovens where they were burned to ash. Auschwitz officials boasted they could process as many as twelve thousand people per day.

Daily Life in the Camps

About 80 percent of Jews arriving at Auschwitz went directly to the gas chambers. Other prisoners who survived selection at the train station marched to buildings where guards took away their possessions.

The huge ovens used by the Nazis for burning the bodies of their Jewish victims.

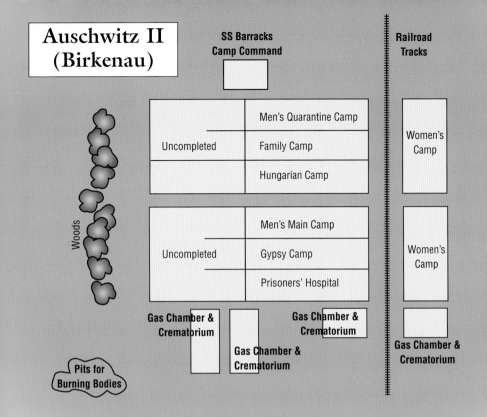

Auschwitz II (Birkenau)

SS Barracks / Camp Command

Railroad Tracks

Woods

Uncompleted	Men's Quarantine Camp
	Family Camp
	Hungarian Camp

Women's Camp

Uncompleted	Men's Main Camp
	Gypsy Camp
	Prisoners' Hospital

Women's Camp

Gas Chamber & Crematorium

Gas Chamber & Crematorium

Gas Chamber & Crematorium

Gas Chamber & Crematorium

Pits for Burning Bodies

Their heads were shaved, they received striped prison uniforms, and numbers were tattooed on their arms. Primo Levi, a survivor of Auschwitz, later wrote, "Nothing belongs to us any more; they have taken away our clothes, our shoes, even our hair; if we speak, they will not listen to us, and if they listen, they will not understand. They will even take away our name."[4]

Each morning before dawn, a whistle blew, telling prisoners they had thirty minutes to dress, wash, and eat breakfast. Most slept in their clothes because few had blankets. Washing was difficult because hundreds in each barracks shared only a few water faucets. Breakfast was usually a piece of bread and sometimes a pint of watery turnip soup.

Then everyone lined up in the camp's central courtyard for roll call. This often took an hour, and they were not allowed to move. Guards wanted to be

Two barefoot concentration camp prisoners peer through a barbed wire fence.

sure no one had tried to escape during the night. They also wanted to count prisoners who had died in their bunks. Roll call was a dangerous time for prisoners. Sometimes, guards chose weaker inmates for the gas chambers, or shot prisoners for minor offenses, such as not standing at attention.

Working Inmates to Death

If prisoners survived roll call, they went to work. Those with special skills—for example, machine operators, steel workers, and electricians—went to camp factories. Others worked in rock quarries, camp kitchens, or laundries. Some helped build more barracks. Some sorted through mountains of suitcases, clothes, eyeglasses, jewelry, and shoes taken from the dead. Some helped process those victims, pulling them out of the gas chambers, searching them, and dragging them to the ovens or to the burial pits.

For lunch, workers received more watery soup. In the evening, after a long day of work and almost no rest, they marched back to their barracks. Another roll call, again lasting more than an hour, took place. During this roll call, if anyone was missing, prisoners were ordered to remain in line until they were found. Once, at Buchenwald, the entire camp had to remain lined up for nineteen hours until two men who had hidden were found.

Hard work, little food, cruel treatment, and extreme heat and cold soon took their toll on prisoners. In most camps, few workers lasted more than a

A group of starving prisoners lines up for another day's roll call.

few months before they were too weak to continue. Despite harsh conditions and a lack of hope, though, some Jews did fight back against Nazi forces that held them captive.

Chapter Three

Fighting Back

Jewish **resistance** to Nazi cruelty took many forms. It ranged from small, secret acts of defiance to open, armed rebellion. When anti-Jewish laws first forced Jewish businesses and synagogues to close, many Jews ignored the law. They conducted business in secret and worshiped in their homes. When Jewish children could no longer attend school, their parents taught them at home. When Nazis began arresting Jews and sending them to the camps, many others went into hiding.

Some Jews joined organized bands of fighters in remote forests. These groups became known as the Resistance. They attacked Nazis whenever and wherever they could. They blew up bridges and railroad tracks, cut telephone wires, and ambushed troops. In ghettos and concentration camps, Jewish prisoners defied orders by smuggling food, holding religious ceremonies in secret, attempting escape, blowing up buildings, and killing guards.

Jewish resistance fighters, armed with machine guns, help in the war against the Nazis.

Some non-Jews also fought back against Hitler's Final Solution. Many hid Jews in their homes, gave them food, or helped them escape to other countries. Some risked their lives to help, were caught, and sent to the death camps along with the Jews.

With Little Hope, Why Fight Back?

Against the overwhelming power of Nazi Germany, it may seem hard to understand why Jews fought back. After all, how could they expect to succeed? At first, people resisted because they did not know how powerful the Nazis would become. They also could not imagine how brutal Nazis would be toward them and those who tried to help them. By the time World War II began, Nazis seemed all-powerful. Yet, resistance continued.

Most Jews during the war knew they could not free themselves from Nazi control. After all, they had few weapons, no powerful allies, and nowhere to run. Instead, they fought for their own dignity. They wanted to make sure their deaths had meaning. They also hoped the world would learn what had happened to them. Survival became the strongest form of resistance. Their goal was to live long enough to tell others what the Nazis had done.

Into Hiding

For many Jews in Germany and other countries controlled by the Nazis, survival meant hiding. If they went out in public, they feared being turned over to the police. Some non-Jewish friends and neighbors built secret rooms in their houses, often in the attic or in the cellar. False walls, secret doors, and hidden tunnels led to these hiding places. In rural areas, some farmers built shacks where Jews could hide. Jews also hid in barns, chicken houses, cellars, and storage huts. Some Jewish parents, knowing they were about to be sent away, gave their children to non-Jewish families to be raised.

One of the best-known cases of hiding Jews from Nazis took place in the Netherlands. With the help of

Anne Frank (left) gave her friend Hannah Goslar Pick (right) the code name "Lies" in her famous diary.

non-Jewish friends, thirteen-year-old Anne Frank and her family went into hiding in a secret apartment above a workshop in Amsterdam in the summer of 1942. They lived there for two years. During that time, Anne kept a diary. She described their daily routine and what she observed on the streets outside. She wrote, "The world has been turned upside down. The most decent people are being sent to concentration camps, prisons, and lonely cells, while the lowest of the low rule over young and old, rich and poor."[5] In 1944 someone betrayed the Frank family and turned them in. Anne died the following year in the Bergen-Belsen concentration camp in northern Germany. After the war, her father found her diary and published it.

Armed Resistance

Many Jews in the ghettos and the camps refused to accept their fate without a fight. To them, escape was the only way to survive. Sometimes, prisoners tried to sneak out or tunnel out, but they were usually captured and killed. At other times, prisoners took up arms against their captors and tried to fight their way out. Such armed revolts took place in more than forty ghettos and in four of the death camps.

A diagram shows the rooms of the house where Anne Frank and her family hid for two years.

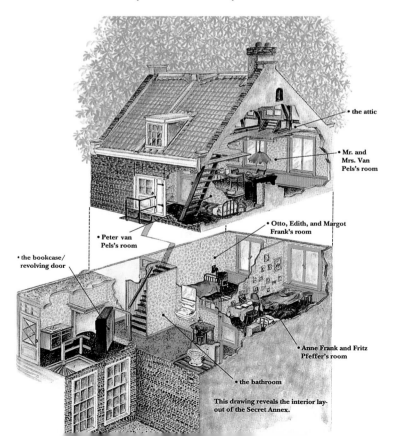

- the attic
- Mr. and Mrs. Van Pels's room
- Otto, Edith, and Margot Frank's room
- Peter van Pels's room
- the bookcase/ revolving door
- Anne Frank and Fritz Pfeffer's room
- the bathroom

This drawing reveals the interior layout of the Secret Annex.

The most famous occurred in the Warsaw ghetto. On January 18, 1943, Jewish leaders refused Nazi attempts to select another five thousand for transport to Treblinka. Armed with only a few pistols, rifles, and hand grenades, nearly twelve hundred Jews held off Nazis forces for four weeks. Some escaped, but most were killed when Nazis stormed in with tanks, destroying the ghetto. Survivors of the revolt were sent to the death camp. Although unsuccessful, the Warsaw ghetto uprising showed Jewish courage and heroism. Word of this heroic stand spread to other ghettos and camps in Germany and Poland, inspiring further resistance.

In the concentration camps, resistance seemed almost impossible. Starvation and overwork made most prisoners too weak to fight. Even under such conditions, uprisings took place. In Treblinka in August 1943, desperate prisoners took weapons from the camp arsenal, killed some guards, and set fire to camp buildings. About 150 escaped, but most were captured. In October 1943, Jewish prisoners at Sobibor attacked camp guards with knives and axes. About 300 escaped. In Auschwitz, late in 1944, prisoners stole explosives from the camp arsenal. They blew up Crematory IV, one of the buildings used to burn bodies. The explosion destroyed the building, but few prisoners escaped.

Non-Jewish Heroes

Outside the camps and ghettos, some non-Jews worked to save Jews from the gas chambers. One famous rescue took place in the small French village of Le Chambon. There, between 1941 and 1944, two pastors convinced villagers to take in Jews who were running from the Nazis. Thousands of Jews were hidden there, or helped out of the country.

A similar rescue took place in Denmark in 1943. When Germany invaded the country, Danes vowed to protect their eight thousand Jewish citizens. Before Jews could be sent to concentration camps, the Danish people organized a fleet of fishing boats and helped them escape to Sweden.

In other countries controlled by the Germans, some people went to great lengths to protect Jews. Chiune Sugihara, an official of the Japanese government,

Danish citizens overturn a German prison van, rescuing Jews headed for a concentration camp.

saved more than thirty-five hundred Jews by giving them papers they needed to leave Europe. Raoul Wallenberg, a Swedish diplomat, saved thousands of Hungarian Jews by issuing them Swedish passports so they could escape to Sweden.

Father Bruno Reyenders, a Belgian priest, organized a network of homes, convents, and monasteries to hide Jews. His efforts saved more than three hundred, including two hundred children. German businessman Oskar Schindler built a factory employing more than one thousand Jewish workers. He told Nazi officials he had to have them because of their skills. His

In a scene from *Schindler's List,* Oskar Schindler (left, portrayed by Liam Neeson) works with Itzhak Stern (portrayed by Ben Kingsley) on a plan to save the lives of Jewish workers.

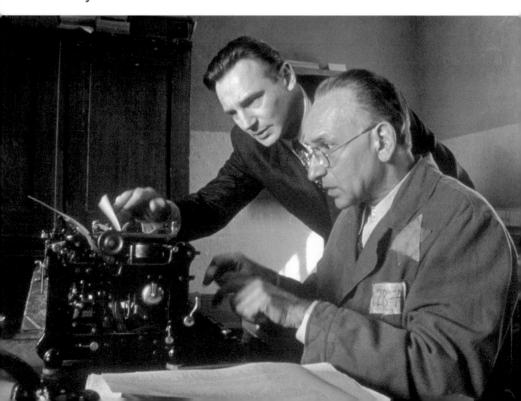

story was told in the 1993 movie *Schindler's List,* which is based on the book by the same name.

These people and countless others risked their lives to save Jews from the death camps. After the war, many Holocaust survivors honored their efforts by naming them Righteous Among the Nations. Thousands of people have received this high honor. Honoring heroes, though, was only one part of the process of healing wounds inflicted by Nazi Germany.

Chapter Four

Liberation, Justice, and Remembrance

The outside world did not learn firsthand about the horrors of the Holocaust, or the bravery of those who tried to help the Jews, until after World War II. Once the war was over, the **Allies** (England, France, the Soviet Union, and the United States) faced several problems. They had to save as many Jewish prisoners as possible. Then, they had to decide what to do with Nazi officers and soldiers who had committed such horrible acts. Finally, they wanted to help Jews recover, and help to provide a safe place for them to live. Jews around the world also wanted to honor those who died during the Holocaust.

Trying to Destroy the Evidence

By late 1944, Germany's defeat seemed certain. Nazis tried to hide what they had done by tearing

Jewish prisoners cheer as Allies liberate them from a
concentration camp.

down some of the death camps. Besides destroying
buildings, Nazis ordered the remaining bodies of
their victims burned. They dug up and burned thousands of bodies that had been buried in mass graves.

Once this was done, they planted grass on the sites
of the camps, to make it seem as though the camps
had never existed. Next, the Nazis forced prisoners to
march hundreds of miles through the snow, back to

Germany. On these death marches, thousands of Jews died.

Liberation of the Camps

Despite their efforts, Nazis could not hide all they had done at the death camps. Near the Polish city of Lublin, the Soviet army **liberated** the first of these camps. This took place at Majdanek in July 1944. Only a few survivors remained. A few months later, on January 27, 1945, the Soviets reached Auschwitz. They found seven thousand survivors, including Anne Frank's father, Otto. Soldiers also found buildings containing 830,000 women's coats and dresses, 348,000 men's suits, 38,000 pairs of men's shoes, and 7 tons of human hair, taken from Jewish victims.

Allied forces, advancing toward Berlin, found other camps. On April 11, 1945, Americans entered Buchenwald, near Weimar, Germany. Soldiers discovered mounds of dead bodies, tools of torture, and twenty-one thousand prisoners, barely alive. Battle-hardened soldiers were shocked by what they saw. On April 15, 1945, British forces entered Bergen-Belsen. They found so many unburied bodies they had to use a bulldozer to bury them.

Food, Water, Medicine, and a New Home

At every camp, the Allies' first task was to provide immediate care for starving prisoners. They provided fresh water for drinking and bathing. They also

A gruesome sight greeted Allied soldiers who entered the concentration camps. They saw row after row of Jewish dead.

brought in food, but many Jews were too weak to eat. Some ate too much and died.

When former prisoners had regained their strength, they wanted to go home. Many, however, had no home to return to. Most of these **refugees**, numbering about 250,000, later settled in the United States, Western Europe, South America, Australia, or South Africa. Others moved to the ancient Jewish homeland, known at the time as Palestine.

Around the world, people who learned about the Holocaust felt ashamed and guilty that it could have happened. Sympathy for Europe's Jews led nations to call for the establishment of an independent Jewish country. A portion of Palestine became that country on May 14, 1948. Known from that time forward as Israel, the new nation welcomed thousands of European Jews.

The Nuremberg Trials
While former concentration camp prisoners were being cared for, the Allies turned their attention to Nazi

Liberated Jewish refugees travel by boat from Europe to Israel.

cruelty. In war, death and suffering are expected. What the Nazis had done went far beyond the normal scope of war. It was a crime.

Proof of mass murder, slave labor, and torture in the camps shocked the world. Hitler had killed himself on April 30, 1945, while Allied forces closed in on Berlin, but many Nazi officers and soldiers who took part in the Holocaust were captured. On November 20, 1945, war crimes trials began in Nuremberg, Germany. These trials lasted until 1949.

Nazis were charged with many different crimes. Most, though, were charged with murdering, mistreating, or enslaving civilians for religious, racial, or political reasons.

Since the Nuremberg Trials, other Nazis who escaped Germany at the end of the war have been hunted down and tried. Nazi hunters, such as Simon Wiesenthal, a survivor of Buchenwald, have devoted their lives to bringing Nazi war criminals to justice. Their search continues.

Honoring the Millions

With the war over, and recovery efforts under way, all that remained was to honor the dead. Family, friends, and others wanted to make sure the world would never forget the Holocaust.

To honor the dead and those who fought to save them, many nations have built monuments. Memorials have been built on the sites of some concentration camps in Germany and Poland. In Israel, a national

On Holocaust Remembrance Day people stop in the streets of Jerusalem for two minutes of silence to honor the 6 million Jews killed in the Holocaust.

Holocaust center, Yad Vashem, opened in Jerusalem in 1953. Besides museums and memorials, it contains a research center for studying Jewish culture. It also honors victims of the Holocaust and heroes of the Resistance.

The United States Holocaust Memorial Museum opened in 1993 in Washington, D.C. More than any other museum in the world today, it brings the memory of the Holocaust to life. Visitors can experience the Holocaust through films, audio recordings, and computer programs. They can walk through reconstructed buildings from the era and see thousands of photographs and items taken from the camps. At the museum's dedication ceremony, Elie Wiesel said:

> For the dead and the living, we must bear witness. For not only are we responsible for the memories of the dead, we are also responsible for what we are doing with those memories. . . . We could not save those who died, but we can save them from dying again, because to forget is to kill them again.[6]

Some survivors and their children have formed organizations to keep the memory alive. In June 1981, more than six thousand survivors from around the world met in Jerusalem. U.S. groups, such as the American Gathering of Jewish Holocaust Survivors and One Generation After, sponsor meetings and special events to remember the Holocaust. A national holiday in Israel, *Yom ha-Sho'ah*, or Holocaust Remembrance Day, honors those who died and those who risked their lives to save them.

Harvey Meyeroff, chairman of the United States Holocaust Memorial Council, also spoke at the dedication of the United States Holocaust Memorial Museum. In his speech, he challenged listeners:

> This building tells the story of events that human eyes should never have seen once, but

President Clinton (center) assists in lighting an eternal flame during the dedication ceremony for the United States Holocaust Memorial Museum in Washington, D.C.

having been seen, must never be forgotten. Our eyes will always see, our hearts will always feel, but it is not sufficient to remember the past. We must learn from it.[7]

Notes

Introduction: Hitler's Plan

1. Quoted in John Toland, *Adolf Hitler*. Garden City, NY: Doubleday, 1976, p. 122n.

Chapter One: One-Way Ticket to the Camps

2. Elie Wiesel, *Night*. New York: Bantam Books, 1960, pp. 13–14.

Chapter Two: Life and Death in the Camps

3. Quoted in Peter Jennings and Todd Brewster, *The Century*. New York: Doubleday, 1998, p. 265.
4. Quoted in Otto Friedrich, *The Kingdom of Auschwitz*. New York: HarperCollins, 1982, p. 35.

Chapter Three: Fighting Back

5. Quoted in David Aretha, ed., *The Holocaust Chronicle: A History in Words and Pictures*. Lincolnwood, IL: Publications International, 2001, p. 506.

Chapter Four: Liberation, Justice, and Remembrance

6. *The Holocaust: In Memory of Millions*. Bethesda, MD: Discovery Productions, 1994. Documentary film.
7. *The Holocaust: In Memory of Millions*.

Glossary

Allies/Allied forces: Countries that banded together to fight against Nazi Germany and Japan in World War II.

anti-Semitic: Hatred of Jews.

crematory ovens: Special ovens built to burn dead bodies to ash.

ghettos: Areas of a city where Jews were required to live. Today, a usually poor neighborhood where people of the same race or religion live.

Final Solution: Nazi term for their plan to kill Europe's Jews.

liberated: Setting someone free.

refugees: People who are forced to leave their home because of war, persecution, or natural disaster.

resistance: Fighting back.

synagogues: Buildings used by Jewish people for worship and religious study.

Zyklon B: Poison gas used to kill people in Nazi death camp gas chambers.

For Further Exploration

Books

Phillip Brooks, *The United States Holocaust Memorial Museum.* Danbury, CT: Childrens Press, 1997. Discusses the United States Holocaust Memorial Museum, from planning to completion.

Jamie Daniel, Michael Nicholson, and David Winner, *Raoul Wallenberg: One Man Against Nazi Terror.* Milwaukee: Gareth Stevens, 1992. Short biography of Wallenberg and his efforts to save Jews.

Anne Frank, *Anne Frank: The Diary of a Young Girl.* New York: Doubleday, 1952. The diary of a teenage girl who hid from the Nazis for two years in the Netherlands before being caught and sent to Auschwitz.

Michael Pariser, *Elie Wiesel: Bearing Witness.* Brookfield, CT: Millbrook Press, 1994. A short biography of the camp survivor, author, and Nobel Peace Prize winner.

Andrea Warren, *Surviving Hitler: A Boy in the Nazi Death Camps.* New York: HarperCollins, 2001. Personal memoir of Jack Mandelbaum, a Holocaust survivor. Excellent introduction to years before and during the Holocaust, combining first-hand accounts with objective narrative.

Websites

The Holocaust Chronicle (www.holocaustchronicle. org). An online version of an encyclopedia of the Holocaust. Thousands of facts, hundreds of pictures, and a complete time line can be found on this site.

Israel's Holocaust Museum and Research Center (www.yad-vashem.org.il). The museum houses the world's largest archive of Holocaust information— 58 million pages of documents, 100,000 photographs, and thousands of filmed testimonies of survivors. Visitors to the website can look at thousands of historical photographs, artwork from the camps, and pictures of museum items. Also includes a section called "No Child's Play," showing the world of children during the Holocaust.

United States Holocaust Memorial Museum (www.ushmm.org). A virtual tour of the largest Holocaust museum in the world. Besides the pictures and text of the museum's exhibits, visitors can learn about hundreds of specific children and adults who died in the camps.

Index